PRACTICE WHAT YOU PREACH

Mariah Claiborne

Copyright © 2025 by Mariah Claiborne

All rights reserved. This book or any portion thereof may not be reproduced or used in any manner whatsoever without the express written permission of the publisher except for the use of brief quotations in a book review.

Printed in the United States of America

First Edition, 2025

PAPERBACK ISBN: 979-8-3482-7756-7
EBOOK ISBN: 979-8-3482-7757-4

Red Pen Edits and Consulting
www.redpeneditsllc.com

TABLE OF CONTENTS

Dedications *1*

Introduction *3*

CHAPTER 1
It's Okay to Believe While Blind *5*

CHAPTER 2
I Don't Like What I Need *11*

CHAPTER 3
Suddenly Takes Time *17*

CHAPTER 4
Gradual Release *23*

CHAPTER 5
Hear the Sound, Obey the Command *31*

CHAPTER 6
Trust the Wind *37*

References *43*

About The Author *45*

DEDICATIONS

To my Pastor, Bill Russell Jr.,

Thank you for seeing me—not just as I was, but for where I was going. Your unwavering belief, guidance, and commitment to pour into me have shaped me into the leader, preacher, and believer I am today. I have had the privilege of getting to know your heart toward the things of God, and I deeply admire the patience and love you effortlessly extend to those around you. You have always sought to understand me through an unfiltered lens and pushed me to grow into who God has called me to be.

Your lasting impact on my life and countless others is a testament to your faithfulness, wisdom, and love for God's people. This book is a reflection of the seeds you've sown, and I pray it honors the legacy of your leadership and your heart.

With deepest gratitude and respect,

Mariah Claiborne

INTRODUCTION

The phrase, "Practice what you preach." It's a simple saying, yet it carries a heavy truth: belief without action is incomplete. It's one thing to talk about faith, trust, and perseverance, but another thing entirely to live them out when life feels uncertain, prayers go unanswered, and the promises of God seem slow to unfold.

Honestly, I've been there—saying the right words, but wrestling silently with my doubts. It's easy to preach about trusting God when everything is going well, but what happens when His process stretches longer than expected? I've learned that faith isn't just something we talk about; it's something we practice. It's choosing to believe when the outcome is unclear and to walk forward when you feel weak. Each chapter of this book explores moments when we're called to do just that—to put our faith into action, even when it's uncomfortable.

This journey isn't about perfection. It's about transformation—growing through the waiting, the wandering, and the wins. I don't write these words as someone who has mastered it all, but as someone who is still learning to practice what I preach. My prayer is that as you read, you'll be encouraged to do the same. Trust the process, because on the other side of practicing what you preach is a life that reflects not just what you say, but who you know God to be.

Let's begin.

Chapter 1

IT'S OKAY TO BELIEVE WHILE BLIND

> ⁶ *When he had thus spoken, he spat on the ground, and made clay of the spittle, and he anointed the eyes of the blind man with the clay,*
>
> ⁷ *And said unto him, Go, wash in the pool of Siloam, (which is by interpretation, Sent.) He went his way therefore, and washed, and came seeing.*
>
> ***JOHN 9:6-7***

Believing without seeing can feel like an impossible task. Faith often requires us to move forward when the way ahead is unclear. But what if this very uncertainty is part of our divine assignment? Sometimes, the hardest lesson is understanding that God, who knows all, calls us to act as if we do too—not because He expects us to know everything, but because He expects us to trust Him completely.

There's a tension we all experience: wanting clarity before we begin. I call this *initial sight*—the desire to see the whole picture before taking the first step. It feels like a necessity, but often it's a luxury. More often than not, we're called to move forward without it. And when we are, it's a call to trust that God's plan for us is greater than what we can perceive in the moment.

I remember a lesson in faith from when I was eight. My dad asked if I was saved, and with confidence, I said yes. He asked how I knew, and I confidently replied that I believed Jesus died for our sins and rose again. Looking back, I marvel at how unwavering my belief was, even at such a young age. But over the years, I learned that experiences alone, while affirming, weren't enough to fully validate my faith. My confidence in God had to grow beyond feelings and into understanding—an understanding rooted in His Word and His promises.

This realization is what strengthens us to lead others. To guide someone to Christ, we must know and trust the path ourselves, even when the steps feel uncertain. And in this journey, the Bible becomes our anchor, reminding us that no matter where we are, the testimony of Christ unites us all.

Take, for example, the blind man in **John 9**. Born blind, his life seemed an enigma to others, who assumed his condition was the result of sin. Yet, Jesus explained that his blindness wasn't punishment but an opportunity for God's glory to be revealed. It's a reminder that the things we struggle with often have a higher purpose—one that is not about us, but about how God works through us. The blind man's healing is a powerful illustration of faith. Jesus made mud with His spit, placed it on the man's eyes, and told him to wash in the pool of Siloam. Here's the part that challenged me: Jesus told a blind man to go to a place he couldn't see. Why not heal him on the spot? Why require such a seemingly impossible step?

But then it hit me…

Sometimes God asks us to move without seeing because He knows we need the journey as much as we need the destination. The mud wasn't just a tool for healing—it was a barrier that ensured the man stayed on course, trusting in the process, not just the outcome. Imagine if the blind man had been healed halfway to the pool. Would he have turned back, thinking the journey was no longer necessary? God often works like this in our lives. He covers what we think we need to see so we don't abandon the path He's laid before us. The healing might start along the way, but the fullness of what He has for us is waiting at the destination.

It's easy to grow frustrated when God sends us on a path that feels beyond our ability. But those moments are precisely when faith grows strongest. The blind man's story reminds us that sometimes believing blindly is not just part of the process—it's the whole point. Faith is not about having all the answers. It's about trusting the One who does. Believing while blind prepares us for the reward of faith: sight. And when that sight comes, it's not just about seeing what's ahead but testifying to the God who carried us through when we couldn't see at all.

So, if you're wrestling with where God has sent you, unsure how to reconcile the deficits you feel with the assignment before you, remember this: faith isn't the absence of sight—it's the courage to believe before it comes. And when you do, you'll not only reach the destination; you'll be able to look back and see how God's hand was guiding you all along.

Chapter 2
I DON'T LIKE WHAT I NEED

> *⁹ And he dreamed yet another dream, and told it his brethren, and said, Behold, I have dreamed a dream more; and, behold, the sun and the moon and the eleven stars made obeisance to me.*
>
> *¹⁰ And he told it to his father, and to his brethren: and his father rebuked him, and said unto him, What is this dream that thou hast dreamed? Shall I and thy mother and thy brethren indeed come to bow down ourselves to thee to the earth?*
>
> *¹¹ And his brethren envied him; but his father observed the saying.*
>
> **GENESIS 37: 9-11**

Most of us can remember being kids, wanting everything we didn't need: dessert before dinner, playtime over homework, and staying up on school nights. It was as if we were drawn to our wants over our needs. Our parents, though, had a different view—they knew what we needed long before we understood it.

As I look back now, it becomes clear that life is often a series of these moments, times when we're called to trust the unseen, to walk into what we can't yet understand, and to give what feels beyond us. Joseph, son of Jacob, faced this lesson early on. He was favored and deeply loved, yet that love brought him more trouble than comfort. His brothers watched as their father's preference grew, and each display of favor only fueled their resentment. Then, Joseph had his dreams. In one of them, he was binding grain with his brothers, but his bundle stood tall while theirs bowed around him. When he shared it, their resentment turned to something darker. A second dream came, with the sun, moon, and eleven stars bowing to him. Though he knew it might only deepen their anger, he couldn't hold back and shared it again. Even Jacob was taken aback. "What kind of dream is that?" he asked, struggling to believe he'd ever bow to his son. Yet, he couldn't entirely dismiss it. Somewhere within, he pondered its meaning, sensing perhaps it was more than just a child's imagination.

Joseph's choice to share his dreams, even knowing how they might be received, speaks to something profound. He wasn't unaware of his brothers' hatred; he knew full well the risk. Yet, something greater urged him on—a need to release what he'd been given, regardless of others' acceptance. I think of all the times we're called to speak or act in ways that feel uncomfortable or inconvenient. Joseph's experience points to a hard truth: we don't get to choose who might need what we have to give. Often, the people most in need of our words, our love, or our support are the hardest to be around. We'd rather avoid them and seek comfort among those who understand us. But sometimes, God's calling pulls us toward the very people we'd prefer to sidestep. In Luke, we read, "Love your enemies, do good to those who hate you, bless those who curse you, pray for those who mistreat you." This takes maturity, a heart willing to see that those who oppose us may need what only we can give.

Jesus shared a parable about a sower scattering seed on different types of ground. Often, we think of ourselves as the sower, but sometimes we're the ground—the ones meant to receive. Joseph's family shows us how different "soil" receives God's Word.

There's the rocky ground, where the seed springs up but quickly withers without depth. This reminds me of Jacob—loving but resistant, unable to let the word truly take root. How many times do I respond this way, welcoming what fits my view but resisting what doesn't?

Then, there's the thorny soil, where weeds choke out the seed. This soil reminds me of Joseph's brothers. They grew up with him, familiar with his face and ways, but couldn't accept his dreams. They were fine with him as long as he stayed on their level, but when his dreams suggested otherwise, their jealousy grew like thorns, suffocating his promise.

Finally, there's the good soil—the heart ready to receive, letting God's word take root and bear fruit. Joseph was like this. Despite all the resistance, he trusted God's plan. His path wasn't smooth. It was marked by betrayal, suffering, and hardship. But he let the promise grow, and in time, it bore fruit.

Wisdom isn't always easy. True wisdom often comes through what stretches us. It's human to resist what we can't control. Proverbs reminds us,

"Get wisdom, though it costs all you have; get understanding." Sometimes, wisdom comes wrapped in discomfort or difficulty. Later, during a famine, Joseph—the one dismissed by his family—held the key to their survival. His vision wasn't just a prediction; it was provision. But for it to bear fruit, it first had to be planted in rocky and thorny ground. Joseph's story reminds me not to dismiss what I don't understand. Let's not be quick to reject what doesn't fit our expectations. We may not control how others receive us, but we can cultivate our hearts to be good soil, ready to receive whatever God has to say—even when it comes in unexpected ways.

Chapter 3
SUDDENLY TAKES TIME

> ⁴² *For he had one only daughter, about twelve years of age, and she lay a dying. But as he went the people thronged him.*
>
> ⁴³ *And a woman having an issue of blood twelve years, which had spent all her living upon physicians, neither could be healed of any,*
>
> ⁴⁴ *Came behind him, and touched the border of his garment: and immediately her issue of blood stanched.*
>
> **LUKE 8:42-44**

Have you ever met someone who always brings every conversation back to God? It doesn't matter if you're talking about work, family, or the weather—they somehow find a way to make it about Jesus. I used to find people like that exhausting.

Not because they were wrong, but because I didn't understand them. It felt like they were doing too much, trying to fit God into everything. Then one day, I became one of them.

Many of us wrestle with waiting on God while holding on to the promise of sudden change. Sometimes, you can pinpoint the exact moment when things shifted: when what used to tempt you no longer held your attention, when old habits lost their grip, or when God worked something in you that felt instantaneous. But if you're honest, that "sudden" moment often took years. It took tears, heartbreaks, and trials to get there. It's the journey that prepares you for the moment. It's why we can do things that seem foolish to the world—like giving generously when we have little or stepping out on faith without knowing the outcome. These actions don't make sense to a natural mind, but they make perfect sense to a spiritual one. As Paul said in **1 Corinthians 2:14**, *"The natural man does not receive the things of the Spirit of God, for they are foolishness to him; nor can he know them, because they are spiritually discerned."* In other words: Spirit recognizes spirit.

Sometimes, we look back and realize that what felt like an instant change was actually a long journey. I remember when God changed my heart and cleaned up my foul language. It felt sudden, but in reality, it was years in the making. I just didn't see all the work happening behind the scenes. To be honest, I would have probably gone back to doing a lot of ungodly things if it hadn't taken me some time to get to where I am. That time was necessary—it shaped me, refined me, and kept me tethered to something greater than myself. For some of us, blessings have been delayed not because God is withholding them, but because of our own unwillingness to fully commit, to make up our minds and genuinely desire the will of God for our lives. We had to endure the furnace, to be tried and tested, just so we could emerge without even a hint of smoke on us.

Let's look at **Luke 8:42-44** - *"For he had an only daughter about twelve years of age, and she was dying. But as He went, the multitudes thronged Him. Now a woman, having a flow of blood for twelve years, who had spent all her livelihood on physicians and could not be healed by any, came from behind and touched* *the border of His garment. And immediately her flow of blood stopped."*

For twelve years, she suffered with an issue of blood. She spent all her money on doctors, endured countless failed treatments, and things only got worse. Her condition didn't just affect her physically; it isolated her. By Jewish law, she was considered unclean and couldn't enter the temple. For twelve years, she lived on the outside, excluded from community and worship. Yet, one day, she heard about Jesus. Something inside her said, "This is it." She pressed through the crowd, disregarding her pain, her failures, and even the law, just to touch the hem of His garment.

But here's what gets me…

What if her healing had come earlier? What if her issue had only lasted twelve days instead of twelve years? Would she have been desperate enough to pursue Jesus with such faith? Sometimes, the length of our trial shapes the depth of our testimony. It's the time spent wrestling, crying, and questioning that leads us to the point of breakthrough. For some of us, God has allowed delays—not as punishment, but as preparation. He's been shaping us, molding us, and strengthening us for the journey ahead. The truth is, suddenly takes time.

When the woman touched Jesus, she was healed immediately. But that twelve-year journey wasn't wasted. Every year of suffering brought her to that moment. **Joel 2:25** says, *"I will restore to you the years that the locust has eaten."* When God moves suddenly, He doesn't just fix the problem; He restores the time that was lost. And it wasn't just about her. Jesus was on His way to Jairus' house to heal his twelve-year-old daughter. The connection isn't a coincidence. Twelve years of suffering for the woman and twelve years of life for the girl—a perfect representation of God's authority and restoration.

The woman's healing wasn't just for her; it was a sign. Her faith set the stage for what Jesus would do next. Here's what I need you to understand: Your journey isn't just about you. When you endure and press through with faith, others benefit. Your testimony becomes someone else's sign of hope. You're not just the one with the issue; you're the one who believes. And because you believe, others will see the signs that follow.

So, if you're still waiting on your suddenly, don't lose heart. God is working, even in the delay. He's restoring the years. He's perfecting what concerns you. And when your suddenly comes, it will be worth every moment you spent waiting.

Chapter 4

GRADUAL RELEASE

And again he entered into Capernaum after some days; and it was noised that he was in the house.

² And straightway many were gathered together, insomuch that there was no room to receive them, no, not so much as about the door: and he preached the word unto them.

³ And they come unto him, bringing one sick of the palsy, which was borne of four.

⁴ And when they could not come nigh unto him for the press, they uncovered the roof where he was: and when they had broken it up, they let down the bed wherein the sick of the palsy lay.

⁵ When Jesus saw their faith, he said unto the sick of the palsy, Son, thy sins be forgiven thee.

⁶ But there was certain of the scribes sitting there, and reasoning in their hearts,

⁷ Why doth this man thus speak blasphemies? who can forgive sins but God only?

⁸ And immediately when Jesus perceived in his spirit that they so reasoned within themselves, he said unto them, Why reason ye these things in your hearts?

⁹ Whether is it easier to say to the sick of the palsy, Thy sins be forgiven thee; or to say, Arise, and take up thy bed, and walk?

¹⁰ But that ye may know that the Son of man hath power on earth to forgive sins, (he saith to the sick of the palsy,)

¹¹ I say unto thee, Arise, and take up thy bed, and go thy way into thine house.

¹² And immediately he arose, took up the bed, and went forth before them all; insomuch that they were

> *all amazed, and glorified God, saying, We never saw it on this fashion.*
>
> ### MARK 2:1-12

There's an assumption many believers carry, though perhaps unknowingly, that when God fulfills a promise, He does so fully and immediately. It's as if we expect Him to drop the entire blessing into our laps in its finished form. While God is certainly capable of doing all things perfectly and completely, His process often doesn't look the way we imagine. Sometimes, His promises are revealed gradually, not because He is limited but because the magnitude of what He is orchestrating involves moving parts beyond what we can see. A gradual release doesn't mean the promise hasn't been made or that it isn't in motion—it simply means God is unveiling it piece by piece, and that can be hard for us to accept.

I'll admit, I've wrestled with this. Not because I don't trust God, but because I trust Him so much that I want the fullness of His promises right away. I've felt this tension deeply in my own life. In March of 2021, I received a prophetic word that God had heard my cry for a child. The promise was clear:

I would have a child. In April, I found out I was pregnant, but just two weeks later, I miscarried. The devastation was overwhelming—not only because of the loss itself but because of the confusion it brought. I had received a word from God, so why didn't it come to pass the way I expected? What do you do when you catch a glimpse of what was promised, but it wasn't the promise itself? When you receive an Ishmael, but God has promised you an Isaac? Sometimes, God places something in front of us not to tease us but to work on the intricate details of His plan. And as hard as it is to admit, the promise is rarely just about us.

This dynamic is evident in **Mark 2**. By this point in His ministry, Jesus had become so well-known that crowds followed Him everywhere He went. In this passage, we see Him teaching in a house that was so packed with people that there wasn't even room near the door. In this setting, a paralyzed man, carried by four of his friends, tried to reach Jesus. But when they arrived, the crowd was impenetrable. Imagine this: God has led you somewhere, but when you arrive, there's no room for you. What happens when the place God sent you feels inaccessible? When the word God gave you feels like it belongs to everyone else too?

The friends of the paralyzed man didn't stop at the door. They looked for gaps and found a way to the roof. In an unconventional and bold act, they lowered their friend through an opening in the roof into Jesus' presence. This teaches us something significant: we need people around us who can see possibilities where others see limitations. Innovative thinkers, those who refuse to accept "no" as the final answer, are invaluable. Sometimes, the breakthrough doesn't come from prior experience but from the faith to try something unconventional.

But here's where the story takes an unexpected turn…

When the man is finally lowered in front of Jesus, Jesus doesn't heal him immediately. Instead, He says, "Son, your sins are forgiven." Imagine being that man. After all the effort to get to Jesus, after allowing his friends to carry him and disrupt someone's roof, Jesus forgives his sins? I imagine the man thinking, But what about my legs? I didn't come here for this.

This moment reveals a hard truth: before God addresses our outward needs, He often begins with the condition of our souls. How often do we ask God for one thing, only for Him to answer in a way that feels adjacent to our request? It's not that God doesn't care about our desires—He does. But He prioritizes what matters most. His work in us often begins inwardly, where healing is most needed, before it manifests outwardly.

The story continues as Jesus discerns the doubt of the scribes who were present. They questioned how He could claim to forgive sins. Addressing their doubts publicly, Jesus asked, "Which is easier: to say, 'Your sins are forgiven,' or to say, 'Get up, take your mat, and walk?'" To demonstrate His authority, He turned to the man and said, "Get up, take your mat, and go home." In that moment, the man was both forgiven and healed.

What stands out here is the way doubt played a role. Doubt didn't stop the miracle; it set the stage for it. God used the scribes' skepticism to showcase His power and authority. This is a reminder that God often works in spaces where belief and unbelief coexist. He uses moments of doubt to reveal Himself in undeniable ways. In other words, doubt attracts miracles. I know that might challenge your thinking, but hear me out. Doubt, when placed in the presence of faith, can actually set the stage for a miracle. This is why we can't insist on only surrounding ourselves with those who think, act, and believe exactly as we do. It's funny, isn't it? The person who doesn't believe never seems to ask, "Who all is going to be there?" But we, as believers, are often the first to question the room. We make excuses like, "Well, my spirit doesn't sit right with just anybody." But could it be that it's time to get to the point where your spirit isn't vexed every time you encounter someone who isn't like you? Don't be so quick to dismiss those who struggle to believe. They might just be the ones you need to unlock your answer.

In the book of John, Jesus says, *"Unless you people see signs and wonders, you will by no means believe."* That verse is profound because it reveals something critical: signs and wonders find those who doubt or don't believe. But they also follow those who do. In other words, the atmospheres most conducive for miracles are those that hold a mix of believers and doubters. In **Mark 2**, I used to wonder why Jesus didn't just forgive the man's sins and heal him all at once. But now I understand. He had to release it gradually, giving room for the doubts in the hearts of the scribes. Not so they would remain hardened, but so God could show Himself mighty and real to everyone present.

Think about that for a moment. What if God is using the doubts of others to amplify the miracle in your life? I've come to thank God not only for the miracles that follow me when I believe, but also for the miracles that find me when I don't. For the times when doubt crept into my own heart or into the hearts of those around me, yet God still chose to show up.

Ultimately, the gradual release of God's promises serves a purpose. It's not just for us—it's for everyone watching. The delayed manifestation of a promise isn't a denial; it's a setup for God to receive glory. Sometimes, we're so focused on what we're waiting for that we miss how God is using our waiting to impact others. His process is intentional. His timing is perfect. The release is happening.

Gradually.

Purposefully.

Perfectly.

Chapter 5

HEAR THE SOUND, OBEY THE COMMAND

⁶ And Joshua the son of Nun called the priests, and said unto them, Take up the ark of the covenant, and let seven priests bear seven trumpets of rams' horns before the ark of the Lord.

⁷ And he said unto the people, Pass on, and compass the city, and let him that is armed pass on before the ark of the Lord.

⁸ And it came to pass, when Joshua had spoken unto the people, that the seven priests bearing the seven trumpets of rams' horns passed on before the Lord, and blew with the trumpets: and the ark of the covenant of the Lord followed them.

⁹ And the armed men went before the priests that blew with the trumpets, and the rereward came

> *after the ark, the priests going on, and blowing with the trumpets.*
>
> *¹⁰ And Joshua had commanded the people, saying, Ye shall not shout, nor make any noise with your voice, neither shall any word proceed out of your mouth, until the day I bid you shout; then shall ye shout.*
>
> ***JOSHUA 6: 6-10***

Have you ever found yourself in a season where growth feels less like progress and more like pressure? I know that feeling all too well. I surrendered my youth to God, and while my peers were learning to navigate life at their own pace, I was being thrust into a process that demanded maturity beyond my years. I call it "uncomfortable maturity." It's a process that doesn't ask for your permission, and the symptoms are often undeniable: frustration, doubt, and the continual death of your own will. This is when you're forced to stretch in ways like watching your words, owning your mistakes, and navigating conversations you would have avoided in another season. Even your relationship with God will change. The dialogues

I have with Him now are deeper and more honest as a result of maturing uncomfortably. And yet, in all this discomfort, I've found gratitude. This season isn't just about claiming victory—it's about perfecting character.

Here's the problem…

We've been trained to celebrate victory while ignoring the beauty of transformation. We celebrate over triumphs but stay silent when someone grows in integrity. Nancy Dufresne once said that there comes a point in your walk with God when you should begin to desire sanctification. That's the place where you stop saying, "They're lucky I'm not who I used to be," and start saying, "I'm grateful for who God is making me."

Joshua, in the book that bears his name, was no stranger to uncomfortable maturity. By the time we reach chapter six, he's leading the Children of Israel through one of their biggest transitions. He's been handed leadership after Moses, crossed the Jordan, and circumcised a new generation that hadn't experienced the old wilderness ways. Now, they stand at the brink of Jericho, a city that God has promised to deliver into their hands. But let's pause right there. God didn't just promise them the city; He gave them the how. And isn't that just like God? If He's talking about the end result, it means you'll survive the process. But the process? That's where the real work happens.

The instructions God gave Joshua were unconventional, to say the least. March around the city once a day for six days with priests blowing trumpets. On the seventh day, march around seven times, then shout after the trumpets blow. Most of us know this story, but here's where we miss it: the trumpets weren't silent for six days. They were blown every day. Can you imagine the confusion that must have caused for the people of Jericho? They had already locked the gates, terrified of Israel. Now, every single day, they hear the sound of war. But war never comes. The sound keeps repeating, but the attack never follows.

God knew what He was doing. The sound wasn't just for Jericho—it was for Israel too. It was a test of trust. Would they be obedient to His instructions, even when the sound made it seem like the time to act was now? This is where so many of us struggle. We hear the sound of opportunity and get anxious. We see the potential for movement and grow impatient. But maturity teaches us that the sound is not the signal; the command is.

Joshua told the people, "Do not shout or make any noise with your voice, nor shall a word proceed out of your mouth, until the day I say to you, 'Shout!'" Joshua understood human nature. He knew that by day four or five, someone might grow weary and start speaking against the process. How often do we do the same? We let frustration creep into our words, and our words sabotage the very promise we're waiting for. We are a reactive people, aren't we? Quick to move, quick to speak, quick to act. But God is teaching us to respond intentionally. You don't need a sign when you've already been given a command. The sound may stir you, but it's the command that sets you in motion. The sound is meant to confuse your enemies, not to dictate your actions. Jericho heard the trumpets and didn't know when or how Israel would strike. The sound unsettled them, while the Israelites stayed grounded in obedience.

I know this firsthand. My husband and I needed more space, so we put our house on the market, believing God for a new home. Less than a mile away sat the house we desired to be ours. It fit the exact description of a prophetic word we received. But there we were, months later, still waiting. And I'll be honest: waiting is hard. The sound of possibility is everywhere, but God's command hasn't come yet.

And still, the lesson remains: Listen to the sound, but obey the command.

This is why you can't afford to move prematurely. The sound may awaken something in you, but your steps must align with His word. Because the truth is, this battle isn't just about you. Your reaction could affect the outcome for everyone connected to you. So wait. Trust. And when the command comes, shout with everything you've got. Because when you've obeyed the process, the promise will not fail. The walls will come down, the victory will be yours, and God will get the glory—not just for the triumph but for the transformation He brought you through on the way.

Chapter 6

TRUST THE WIND

> ^{29} *He giveth power to the faint; and to them that have no might he increaseth strength.*
>
> ^{30} *Even the youths shall faint and be weary, and the young men shall utterly fall:*
>
> ^{31} *But they that wait upon the Lord shall renew their strength; they shall mount up with wings as eagles; they shall run, and not be weary; and they shall walk, and not faint.*
>
> **ISAIAH 40:29-31**

I am what some might call directionally challenged. To put it plainly—I stay lost. If you're someone who gets annoyed by the constant voice of a GPS, I'm not your ideal travel companion. I rely on it heavily, even when I know where I'm going. Why? Because I can't stand the feeling of being lost.

There's something unsettling about not being where you're supposed to be, especially when you don't know how to get there—or worse, how to get back home. That's why the most satisfying moment of any trip for me is hitting the "Home" button on my GPS. There's a certain peace in knowing you're on your way back to where you feel most settled, comfortable, and safe. Many of us are looking at God the same way, saying, *"Lord, I'm ready to get back to a place where I feel grounded."* After seasons of busyness or feeling lost, we crave the good part—the peace, the safety, the homecoming.

This is where the Israelites found themselves in **Isaiah 40**. Captive in Babylon, they were desperate to go home. The chapter begins with a message of hope: a promise from God to bring them back. God reminds them of who He is, saying things like, *"Who else has held the oceans in his hands?"* and, *"Has the Lord ever needed anyone's advice?"* God is essentially saying, *"The Creator of the universe is with you, even in exile, and I'm going to bring you home."*

Then we arrive at verse 29, which says, *"He gives power to the weak and strength to the powerless."* At first, this verse puzzled me. Why wouldn't God give strength to the weak and power to the powerless? It seemed backward. So, I dug deeper. Strength is the ability to exert force—to move ourselves or something around us, like lifting a suitcase. Power, on the other hand, is tied to will—it's the speed and decisiveness with which we apply strength, like catching a falling suitcase. When God says, *"I give power to the weak,"* He's saying that in moments of weakness, what you really need is the *will* to press on. Sometimes, we pray, *"Lord, give me the strength to face this,"* and then we wake up still dreading it. That's because the issue isn't your strength; it's your will.

Then He says, *"I give strength to the powerless."* This means there will be times when you have to move before you're convinced it will work. God gives you the physical ability to take the next step, even when your mind hasn't caught up to what He's doing. Think about the Israelites crossing the Red Sea. God didn't wait for them to be fully convinced before delivering them. He gave them the ability to move forward, even as He worked on their hearts in the wilderness.

Many of us struggle with this because we want God to move in ways that make sense. We want Him to start small, to ease us into things. But sometimes, God throws us into the deep end. Not to harm us, but to teach us to trust Him completely. **Isaiah 40:31** says, *"But those who trust in the Lord will find new strength. They will soar high on wings like eagles. They will run and not grow weary. They will walk and not faint."*

At first glance, the order seems odd. Wouldn't it make more sense to walk first, then run, and finally soar? But God's ways aren't limited by our logic. He's asking for our *best* trust right from the start. Too often, we say, *"Lord, let me ease into trusting You. Let me walk first, then I'll run, and eventually, I'll soar."* But God is saying, *"Trust Me fully, right now."*

Here's the truth…

When you walk or run, your trust is in what you can see—your legs, the ground beneath you. But when you soar, you have to trust the wind. You have to trust what you *cannot* see to carry you where you need to go. Eagles can't soar without the wind. And God never sends us without His wind. Trusting Him means allowing His unseen presence to propel you forward. When we trust the wind of

God, we find a strength that renews us. Soaring takes less energy than walking or running because the wind does the work. This is what it means to "find new strength."

So many of us are frustrated because we've only experienced walking and not fainting, or running and not growing weary. But we've never soared—never allowed the wind of God to carry us fully. God is saying, *"You control your wings; let Me control the wind."* When you trust Him first, you preserve your strength for the journey ahead. What seems hardest—soaring—is actually the easiest because you're relying on Him.

So, whether you're walking, running, or soaring, remember this: the wind is there. You can't see it, but you can feel it pushing you forward. Trust the wind. Let it carry you where God is calling you to be.

REFERENCES

Holy Bible, *King James Version*

ABOUT THE AUTHOR

Mariah Claiborne

Mariah Claiborne was born and raised in Chapel Hill, North Carolina. An experienced educator, she has devoted her career to shaping young minds and fostering a love for learning. Mariah earned her Bachelor of Science in Middle Grades Education (B.S. Ed.) from The University of North Carolina at Greensboro and spent several years teaching mathematics. She is advancing her career in Educational Leadership at High Point University, furthering her passion for inspiring growth both in and out of the classroom.

Beyond her professional career, Mariah serves as an Elder within One Way Churches International and her local church, Harvest City Church in Greensboro. Her life is a beautiful balance of professional excellence, spiritual service, and family devotion. Mariah is a loving mother to Jacob and Chrisette Claiborne and a devoted wife to Marquist Claiborne. She finds her greatest joy in creating a safe, nurturing home and in faithfully fulfilling the roles God has given her.

Mariah's unwavering commitment to education, ministry, and family reflects her character and is a living testament to God's faithfulness in every season of her life.

www.ingramcontent.com/pod-product-compliance
Lightning Source LLC
LaVergne TN
LVHW061042070526
838201LV00073B/5144